a natural
cacophony

a natural cacophony

poems

Sydney Lo

Winner of the 2017
Florence Kahn Memorial Award

National Federation of State Poetry Societies, Inc.
NFSPS Press

A Natural Cacophony
© 2017 by Sydney Lo

Published May 2017
NFSPS Press
National Federation of State Poetry Societies, Inc.
www.nfsps.com

Edit and design by Kathy Cotton
Author's photograph by Jes Campbell

Printed in the United States of America
CreateSpace, Charleston, South Carolina

ISBN-13: 978-1545412602
ISBN-10: 154541260X

CONTENTS

ACKNOWLEDGMENTS

I am incredibly fortunate to have had a myriad of people encourage me to pursue poetry throughout my life. I am so excited to share my chapbook with them, and can only hope that my poems honor the incredible roles they have had in my life.

Thank you to my parents, who loved my poems even when they were just broken limericks made in first grade. You have always supported my passion for poetry, and have helped me realize my literary aspirations. You stayed up with me as I edited poems, shared my excitement over my poetry publications, and reminded me to continue writing. Every word I write holds the echo of your voices.

Thank you to the Grand View Chapter of the League of Minnesota Poets, who welcomed a young, nervous poet all those years ago. Listening to your poems and stories, I am continuously awed by your masterful skills with words. You have inspired and guided my own poetic endeavors, for which I am forever grateful.

Thank you to my English instructors throughout my years of education. Literature is a vast and complex subject, but you persisted with enthusiasm and unending positivity. You showed me the world of poetry, from writing projects to studies of Gwendolyn Brooks, and were always willing to continue discussion long after classes ended. I cherish every moment I spent learning from you.

Thank you to Kathy Cotton, who made this book look so beautiful. Her many hours coordinating with me and crafting every page has made this dream a reality.

Thank you to the National Federation of State Poetry Societies for this extraordinary opportunity. Their various contests and competitions continue to enable the writing of young poets like me, and I am extremely appreciative of their support.

Finally, thank you to wildflowers and Minnesota and the way words sound spoken aloud. I have discovered you again and again, and am transfixed in your idyllic imperfection every time.

Sydney Lo

FOREWORD

Brown University freshman Sydney Lo displays exceptional insight and complexity in this ten-poem collection set solidly in nature and self-revelation. *A Natural Cacophony,* she tells us, shapes reality on a scale of sound and rhythm: each poem exploring her experiences with the natural world, deriving her native Minnesotan landscape from wildflowers, and conversation from dissonance. Lo's poems evolve as expressive connections between grounded objects and delicate abstraction.

Judge Larry Woiwode notes that Lo has a "true original voice, with overtones of Hart Crane and Hopkins; sunk deep in nature in a natural way." Joyce Sutphen, Poet Laureate of Minnesota, adds that the debut book is "filled with some of the most gorgeously textured lines I have ever read in contemporary poetry."

The College Undergraduate Poetry Contest committee is honored to present Lo's first book, the 2017 winner of the National Federation of State Poetry Societies Florence Kahn Memorial Award. We expect to see this young poet's name rise repeatedly to the top.

Kathy Cotton, Editor
May 2017

A Bee Begins with a Singular Sound

A bee is unfurled honeycomb and so creates itself
in assemblage of petals and hexagonal tessellation
in soft bumble suspended by spring breezes.

A bee breathes into clusters of coneflower buds,
body burrowed into the bloom's fragrant isolation.
It becomes static buzzed pollen and plant rustle,
stamen shivers and plumeless seed dispersal,
a splayed breaking of a silent genesis,
as beads of nectar build on the combs of its forelimbs.

From the bee
insect rhythm grows, stuttered hum,
staccato spills into salamanders, dragonflies, shrews,
splits the still beginnings of the plains.

From the bee
bird songs and bison rumbles solidify,
burst outward from prairie undergrowth,
muffle out the creak of cottonwood and cricket chirps
pulled up by wind whistles into the open sky.

From the bee
beings filled with other sounds take shape
pre-metamorphized in stretched sapling branches,
cemented by the thud of their weight against the soil.

From the bee
a human starts to sound out origin,

sets a word to noise, writes sudden emergence,
writes a dichotomy of language.

A bee is collected by their poems, ballads, odes, epics,
prodded by attempts to describe flowered existence,
stanzas of observations and conjecture,
statements of distance and presumption
sound on sounds on sounds drowning out
its sudden abstraction,
its quiet unbecoming.

Spoken

A dialogue sputters, splits,
and I still my head against its discourse—
diaphragm thuds, darkness, redness,
resonance and relentless reason.
I lose conviction of self in its flesh.

With shadow-stilled doubts I reduce
pulsed bronchiole stiffenings
less than intimacy, more than comfort,
warped trachea and exhaled breath,
admonishment then structure of absolution,
conjecture then construction of resolution.

I fill fibrous alveoli with hollowed sound,
hummed cacophony, hardened voice,
mold porous tissue from subliminal statements,
answers, questions, voracious chatter,
begin again my anatomy from the lungs.

I set my ribcage against this swell,
draw my skin from tints of conversation,
become stutters and singular utterances,
physical thoughts and listened moments,
build myself from inside out.

My Response

Only good?

        [Thick-lipped splitting] [One-note discord]
        [Porous delineation] [Slip slipping] [Degree]
        [Indigo as a means of translation]
        [Lascivious meandering] [Hold—Open on]

                I prepare for bentness,
                when I am in the moment vowels,
                and my tongue curls over teeth.
                I make backwards a list
                with polished sense of position,
                with blue ink pen and spit.

Conversation with a Stranger

It is waltzed up and wild,
hollowed of marbled graces,
with watchwords and line rehearsals,
wisdom, whittled notions of worth,
and what was said—what will be
heard in the evening
is weighted,
is the feel of weather at night,
the sky carved in insecurity
with light and light wavered
on the what was once reflective,
what was once a comfort shattered
once and once again
a "will they go" and farther.

Faltered.

Half-assembled in ellipses.

The bluff entanglements shucked
between the who and with the other
statement despite the wedged wills,
water-marked by what is unlearned.

And it is gone, past lacquered glances,
past plaster molds unfolding in its going
when god-forgiven words take hold

and bend within them rhythms,
a corpus callosum of repetition

and what I come to say again.

Through the Country

I find I travel within twelve variations of tar,
pour litany over landscape to make it level,
drive towards, leave for, stop at
a station settled into sameness,
skip along the surface of a country, still movement,
return to the same surroundings every twelve miles,
choose the seat by the window.

{parking lot}
{train station} {half-witnessed blur}
{bloated ditch being} {overpass shadow}
{flashing streetlight intersection}
{train station} {empty roads}
{gas station} {bus station}
{parking lot}

I persist in ruptured exposure,
rescind the gentle press of progression.
I visit station doors,
metal frames and arrival-departures,
knots in a string from A to B,
permutations of going.

I watch my passing evolve in stuttered thuds,
catch glimpses of non-destinations, devoured terrain,
scattered towns, people peering out from the homogeny,
dilapidated homes and dirt roads rotting between fields,
but I never touch a place without intention,
and I never travel beyond the station.

Past Duluth

The hidden driftwood blistered by the shallow water,
the falls, the swift tufts of turning streams, the sea,
the clear depth, the crisp split of lake and land,
the still disrupted, cooled epiphany,
who has followed past the vaulted bridges?
who spilled sediments into the cliffs?
the pebbled indentations, pine sea glass,
the curve of the trail, the centered oak in the gravel,
the bloated underbellies of carp,
kayaks pressed against sand,
the seagulls, the chipped paint on inn signs,
the colonization,
the cabins carved into the woods,
narrow roads between them,
the turquoise moss bloomed beneath us,
grayed along its edge,
and again we walked the shore, autumn wind,
waiting on the other,
on going north, with worlds and agates in our pockets,
the knots in tree roots, the spotted back of loons,
toward hollowed ports, breathing in smoke,
we stumbled on worn palisades bleeding splintered cement,
we stopped, startled the silhouette of a lighthouse,
we grew soft against the chill, did not know another way,
observed a raven's wingspan, crossed the river,
the stones, the uncertain passage, muddied footprints

were we exploring figures? did we lose something in it?
by chance I uncovered the autumn blossom of a marigold,
submerged leaves in the exposed riverbed,
pressed petals against me to stain my skin.

Evening Horticulture

There in the bathtub
with my barely being there,
barely breathing air that was once
a breath for better others
whom I, by chance, will never know
in bubbled silence after dark,

weeds grow.

Weeds grow between frame and floor
beneath what is in moments
twig-rooted in willow branches
or hooked in wilted sapling buds.

And at night I am convinced of rose,
rose on rose that rises by my bed
where if thought it could be my being,
where if willing would make the worse outcome.

At that moment there is more
to bloom and to blued petals,
pulled loose what was held to
until nothing and nothing keeps me
in where and what I am, in why
I cannot manage the water pressing
permutations of droplet forms,

the entirety of its weight against
my skin, again and again
like the rhyme I remember
stuck and stuck inside me
when all that is good and green
about all the things I know
is kept from broken dawn-light
by arched leaves, endless weeds,
is unmade within the garden.

Metamorphosis of a Moth into a Pomegranate

Fold into one another
feathered arches textured by translucence,
stiffened textiles pressed against glass,
winged intricacies of speciation,
scientific nomenclature of a thing.

A homogenous thickness consumes
peeled labels and wire limbs,
coiled proboscis and tightly woven veins,
delicate plumes of antennas,
prized speckled patterns.

The wings
the not wings
the wrapping of
     a beaded thorax,
     a ribbed abdomen molded into spheres
     with skeleton pressed inward,
     flesh-burst from pressure
begins from this reconstruction.

The chrysalis expands with dynamic force,
dent-dyed maroon,
from the amassing of trophic cascades
and systematic adaptation,
from moonlight and mosquito netting.

Seeds of moth body follow
the mitosis of new cosmos,
fill with nectar of forgotten blooms,
and in the wing-shell multiply their pulpy centers,
blushed rind, bloated arils, ripened pips,
with each wound in echo
to the lengthened movement of nocturnal flutter,
to a browned creature pinned to a board,
to what it was.

Final Visit to the Farm

In the dirt I dug out a hole to pour you into.

It filled with phlox and cinquefoil,
the caraway of abandoned fields,
bluestem helixes and history, limp hues,
hyssop, vervain, the burden of your pasture,
lupine blossoms half-trapped in their sepals,
deserted trails, the apple tree by the house,
tilted silos, swallow nests and silence,
harebell blooms, the residue of harvest,
sputtered perforations of aster, spilling out,
the buckled weight of bergamot,
what was left of the barn,
your name, the otherness of rust,
switchgrass growing in metal frames,
stagnant water, deformed chicken wire,
the loosestrife and sorrel, spring pigments,
salt and stones in the soil, the unbroken sky,
the aperture of your belonging,
the severed edge of mounded earth.

This is where I began.
I fiddled with thistle florets and milkweed,
collected decay, slate, dandelion seedlings.
I wrote out what you were.

You said it was enough.

Transitory

I proliferate beyond constraint
with tendrils and arches folded into one another,
small moon shells, marine architecture,
crushed opals, pomegranate fractures,
ivory cartilage and spinal discs,
some of it unknowingly.

Daybreak and bone houses
breathe in the umber of my syllables,
my hacked-up disquiet and abandoned symmetry.
This is like a sense organ expanding in the water.
They say I promised inward heights,
telescopes and ribbed petal shudders.
They say blue-rimmed eyes, stoicism,
prairie cotton, forest diminishment,
secret human loss and kingfisher azure.
They say I ended bent.

I bring that end to the garden,
I decide the pollen fragments and consonant blooms
pull spindled, intentional vowels from crystallic mouth.
I collapse marbled vessels of placement and position,
cubist skeletons, marsh designs, lithe overture,
suffer from predation and accumulation of unsurvival.
This is an incongruity curled into an oval.
This is being born unknown.

Photo by Jes Campbell

As a first-year student at Brown University in Providence, Rhode Island, Sydney Lo became the 2017 winner of the NFSPS Florence Kahn Memorial Award for her manuscript, "A Natural Cacophony." She was also the first-place winner of the Minnesota Manningham Student Poetry Contest for the senior division in 2015. Her poems have been published in *The Catalyst Literary Journal*, *The Round Magazine*, and *The Triangle Literary Anthology*.

Lo is a staff writer for Brown University's *Post-Magazine* and a member of the League of Minnesota Poets. Her writing goals include continuing to develop her skills, engaging in additional statewide and national contests, and publishing a full-length book of poems and a fiction novel. Lo is a native of Sartell, Minnesota.

Larry Woiwode, Poet Laureate of North Dakota, is Writer in Residence at the University of Jamestown, where he teaches creative writing, world literature, contemporary American fiction, and Native American literature. He is the author of the poetry collection *Even Tide* (FSG, 1977) and a chapbook, *Land of Sunlit Ice* (NDSU Press, 2016). His poetry has appeared in *The Atlantic Magazine, Harpers, The New Yorker, Transatlantic Review,* etc., and is reprinted in a dozen anthologies.

His novels include *Beyond the Bedroom Wall*, finalist for the National Book Award and Book Critics Circle Award, and six of his books have been selected as "notable books of the year" by the *New York Times Book Review*. His stories appear in four volumes of *Best American Short Storie*s, and he has published two memoirs, two collections of essays, a commentary on the book of Acts, and a children's book, among others.

2017 CUP WINNERS

Florence Kahn Memorial Award
A Natural Cacophony by Sydney Lo
Brown University, Providence, RI

Edna Meudt Memorial Award
Exhales by Brian Selkirk
University of Arizona, Tucson, AZ

1st Honorable Mention
"My Branch of Theology" by Seth Danleya
Corban University, Salem, OR

2nd Honorable Mention
"Revolution" by Juliana Chang
Stanford University, Palo Alto, CA

3rd Honorable Mention
"In Winter" by Grace Carhart
Gordon College, Wenham, MA

4th Honorable Mention
"8th Grade Notebook" by Alyssia Mingo
Minnesota State University, Moorhead, MN

5th Honorable Mention (Tie)

"She Wonders" by Faith King
University of Wisconsin, Superior, WI

"I have no understanding of the modern world;
and I don't understand anything else"
by Caleb Rosenthal
Lawrence University, Appleton, WI

In 1988 NFSPS planned the addition of a college-level scholarship, subsequently named in memory of NFSPS charter member and past president Edna Meudt. In 1999, with a generous bequest by Florence Kahn, the NFSPS Scholarship Award expanded to include a second competition for the Florence Kahn Memorial Award.

Now named the College Undergraduate Poetry (CUP) Competition, the annual contest is open to students working toward a degree in an accredited U.S. college or university. Winners of the Meudt and Kahn awards each receive $500, publication and 75 free copies of their chapbook, a $300 travel stipend to attend and read at the NFSPS convention, and other perks.

Contest guidelines and submission dates are posted on the NFSPS website, www.nfsps.com.

NFSPS CUP Committee:

Chair, Shirley Blackwell, New Mexico
Editor, Kathy Cotton, Illinois

The National Federation of State Poetry Societies (NFSPS) is a nonprofit organization, exclusively educational and literary. NFSPS offers linguistic and professional contexts that appeal to the mind and spirit and is dedicated to the furtherance of poetry on the national level and to uniting poets in the bonds of fellowship and understanding.

Membership in NFSPS is through membership of any state poetry society affiliated with the Federation (see www.nfsps.com). Poets in states without an affiliated society may join state societies as at-large members.

Poetry competitions sponsored by NFSPS include:
- 50 annual poetry contests with cash prizes totaling more than $6,000, including a grand prize of $1,000.

- Stevens Poetry Manuscript Competition for a full-length poetry collection.

- College Undergraduate Poetry Competition with the Florence Kahn Memorial and the Edna Meudt Memorial awards going to the top two chapbook manuscript winners.

- Manningham Trust Student Poetry Contest for winners advancing from state-level competitions.

- The BlackBerry Peach Awards for Poetry Spoken and Heard Contest for print and spoken-word poetry.

For more information on contests or membership, visit the website, www.nfsps.com.

Made in the USA
Columbia, SC
12 June 2017